LEFTOVERS

Cassandra Atherton

LEFTOVERS

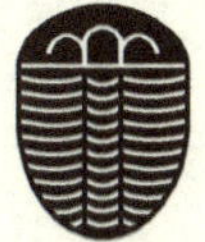

PART I

Carrying a Watermelon

After eighty-five days, I gave birth to a watermelon. It wasn't easy, a full-term jubilee watermelon is forty pounds and this one was delivered breech. When my water broke, it pooled on the floorboards beneath my bare feet. You didn't realise it would travel under the wood and warp the grain. You'd only find that out the following day when you brought the watermelon home; you could feel the edges of the board curving under your toes. By the time you got me to the hospital, I was dilated ten centimetres and the nurse said it was too late for an epidural. But the melon's rind was slick and helped me squeeze it down the birth canal. When I finally pushed it out, I held it in my arms, stroking the skin. "It's perfect," you said sniffing its head, "smells so sweet". It takes a while to stitch me up, so I stay in the hospital while you take the watermelon home. You ring me from the kitchen, swollen boards under your feet, the long-bladed knife in your hand. "Next time, let's try for a cantaloupe," you say.

Eggs

You buy me a Royal Doulton Bunnykins eggcup for Easter—on its side, a picture of anthropomorphic field rabbits sheltering under a red umbrella. Your card says it's to hold my boiled egg upright—for when I dip in the tip of buttery toast soldiers. But I'm not ready to eat your eggs—I don't want to be another of your lovers, served deli-style at your kitchen bench. Instead I imagine that when my egg has cooked for four minutes in your saucepan, you turn and tell me I'm as perfect as that egg. But all I hear is 'First Murderer: What, you egg!' Ovum. Zygote. On Good Friday it rains and you take me to bed—my ovaries greet you, sunny side up.

Pigging Out

for Paul Munden

I like pigs so much that I'm not interested in bringing home the bacon. I'll only eat turkey bacon. My breakfast eggs riding on long, pink rashers. Rushed, rashed, eaten in haste. It's no surprise that *The Three Little Pigs* has always my favourite fairytale and Arnold on *Green Acres* is my dream child. I envy Marie Darrieussecq for her *Pig Tales* and Petunia Pig for being Porky Pig's girlfriend. I've told a lot of porkies but I'm not lying when I tell you I've loved Wilbur and Babe equally. I have a piggy bank, I give piggy backs, I go 'wee, wee, wee all the way home', but my house is a pigsty.

Hygrometry

I want you to age me for sixty days in a cellar and see if I mature. Become stronger. Spicier. Like Saint Agur cheese. Ribbonned with olive green mould, I'll wait in the darkness. My veins reaching for you. Long tributaries of blue. In the humidity I expand, imagining you piercing me as I ripen.

Banana

Once, on a Louisiana plantation we saw bananas growing, like asymmetrical gondolas against a canal of sky. You called them phallic chandeliers while I mourned them flowering and bearing fruit only once. A lone banana is reclusive and introspective but if a hand of them consists of ten to twenty fingers, I am already in their clutches. On our way back to the minibus, you show me the banana heart and I wait to slip on its peel.

Passionfruit

You promised to kiss me with a mouth full of passionfruit pulp; pledged to plunge your tart yellow tongue between my lips, on the longest day of the year. I loiter at your kitchen bench on the summer solstice, with a bowl full of bisected passionfruit, their seeds glistening like tadpole spawn. You begin by sucking the flesh from the wrinkled hemispheres, your sticky fingers coming to rest on my bare leg, a tiny fingerprint arch of amber. I urge you closer, binding us in the xanthous moment. Sun high in the sky, smooth black seeds become stepping stones from your mouth to mine; I tug on the sharp-tasting membrane, but part of it still lies on your tongue. You hike up my skirt. *Passion play,* you breathe.

Neon Ice-cream Cone

My great-grandmother was born with holes in her earlobes. Romany. A caravan child. I remember my childhood of Russian Caravan tea, all lapsang souchong-y. You think Gypsy means Gypsy Rose Lee and regale me with stories of her speaking at union meetings; I wait for the striptease. We run away to Coney Island and I think it's going to be all flashing yellow neon ice-cream cones, but when we take the D train to Brooklyn, my dreams short circuit. The only yellow neon is the zigzag of mustard on the hotdog sign, Nathan's Famous, and you take me to the boardwalk, but not under it. At the sideshow, the bearded lady reads your tea leaves and points out the long plait curling itself around the rim of your cup. You cross her palm with silver and propose to the mermaid in the life-size fish tank.

Pineapple

for Paul Hetherington

Pineapple gives me atlas tongue. But I eat it and travel the world on my tastebuds: pineapple for breakfast in Hawaii with frangipanis and pink ahi poke. I never got to the Dole Plantation, I was busy drinking piña coladas on the beach. There were bags of sweet pineapple rings by the side of the road on our way to Queensland—too many hours in the back seat of my grandfather's yellow Ford, sticky fingers winding down the window and my grandmother passing me tissues. Sweet and sour chicken in Hong Kong was tart and toffee coloured and stained the plate orange. A deconstructed pineapple upside-down cake on your birthday in New York was a disappointing sponge with candied pineapple on the side. You blew the candle out, I ate the sugary pineapple ring. In our apartment I made you the Betty Crocker recipe. You told me to close my eyes, lit a stumpy candle and said I could have your wish.

Fish and Chips

I've never been a happy camper. I never went to band camp, or summer camp, I wasn't at Camp Q or Camp Climax. I hate campervans and I'm no trailblazer. I don't know north from south. I never explore uncharted territory or what lies beyond the edges of the map. But every Boxing Day I'd hammer in tent pegs to anchor my grandparents' annex, holding each one on an acute angle, staking the earth. In those amber afternoons the dragons of my childhood were gobbled up with fish and chips in white butcher's paper.

Biscuit Crumbs

I wonder how I could ever have resisted you, at elevenses, with yo-yo crumbs resting in the corners of your mouth. Those yellow nuggets of biscuit teetering on the edge of your lips. I've never been much of a biscuit eater. I hate Tim-Tams and I spurn the Arnott's Family Assorted, but I don't mind madeleines for their literary taste and langues-de-chat for their felinity. You reach for another yo-yo and I think you must have mistaken elevenses for the number of biscuits you should eat in one go. At noon, when they've all been devoured, you take me to your office. My tongue traces a biscuit trail; I break apart on your lips.

Madeleine

On Friday he left me. He took his purple toothbrush, his tennis socks and his copy of *Remembrance of Things Past.* He didn't wave goodbye. He didn't kiss me. He just left. Because it was Friday. On Sundays we used to spread a tartan blanket beneath a tree and watch the star-filled bats in the Jardin des Plantes. He liked to put his long musicians fingers in my hair when I touched the small, oval callous under his chin and its twin at the base of his neck. I reached for my iPhone and photographed the empty space beside me, all crumpled sheets and missing pillows. I made it my screensaver to remind myself never to date French men who buy their madeleines in bulk.

Doughnut

On the fifth morning, you buy me a jam iced doughnut with hundreds and thousands at the airport. But I'm not ready for closure, I can still feel your hands, now cupping your coffee, cradling my breasts. My absence insinuates itself between us. You embrace me in past tense, stripping your flesh of my scent and returning my heart in a plastic bag. I want to tell you that 'terminal' is a terrible word, but I take a sip of your coffee. When the plane is delayed, I contemplate another doughnut, but the moment has gone. You have your ending.

Cellar

As you sleep, I sneak into your wine cellar; popping the lock with a bobby pin and wiggling the latch free. Huddling into its cool gloom, the cement floor imprints its grid on the balls of my bare feet. Wine racks are wooden catacombs; a temporary holding space. You once told me a lower pH has more ageing potential, so we made love beneath an oak tree. Now, I trace the borders of an empty box and climb inside its darkness. I feel its shape settle into me as I wait for you to taste how round I am on your tongue.

Tequila Slammers

Your lips free float at the bottom of my tequila bottle. Preserved like a worm until the final peg of tequila when they squeeze through the neck of the bottle and smack against mine. On National Tequila Day I take you home and you slither beneath my crisp apple sheets. In the morning between ten and twelve we free float in limpid nectar. Sometimes you tell me my bonny blu eyne are as blue as agave tequilana. Sometimes twa corbies rest on my collarbone and peck out my tongue for you to preserve.

Soft-Shell Crab Haunting

You haunt the cafés in my street; take up residence in rooms filled with breakfast and brunch near my apartment. On dark mornings, I see you sitting at melamine corner tables; your crab-hands scuttering between menu, coffee and phone. I'd join you, but I know if I edge into the corner with you, I'll see your visage is just a trick of light and memory. So, I stand back and remember long nights and easy mornings; the sound of your skin on mine. I leave your ghost in the corner with a soft-shell crab sandwich and order my cup of herbal tea to go.

Dairy

I cut my milk teeth on strawberry frappés, always shaken, never stirred. I spent teenage days sipping milkshake martinis through stripy paper straws, dreaming I was a Bond girl. But seven has never been my lucky number and paper straws eventually become soggy. It was much later I learnt that a glass of milk could save an avulsed tooth. But mine wasn't knocked out, it was grated against gravel as I slid across the tarmac on my lip. Fragments of tooth can't be tucked under a pillow, or put in a jar by the side of the bed for the tooth fairy. In the dulce de leche years, I hold onto my sweet tooth.

Fowl

i.

It started small, the size of a Fruit Tingle. Pearlescent, squishy mini-dome on my right shoulder. Purple in the cold. Salmon-pink in the heat. Say hello to my little friend, I used to say, tugging at the neck of my t-shirt. At sixteen it had grown to the size of a plum. Hard and shiny. I hid it under my hair. Taped some strands to it each morning. In my twenties it was as large as an upside-down flowerpot. But it grew bigger and bigger still. Now, it's the size of a small wheelbarrow. Red and moist. I can't shrug it off. Not even my thick lilac jumper can camouflage its bulk.

ii.

White room. Cream recliner. She cuts a crescent shape and massages my bump. Multilobulated lipoma. As she pushes on my skin, I feel the edge of something dislodge. "Have you been in contact with a prickly edged blue floweret?" she asks. I can't shrug, my shoulder is numb. She slides her finger into the semi-circle of skin and pulls out a pink pom-pom. Her thumb and index finger find a sky-blue neck tie with a thick honey-like stain. Nurses have gathered. A cherry branch is next, I feel its twigs rasp against my skin as she removes it. Inch by inch. Finally, she pulls out white chickens. They peck out the large empty sack in my shoulder and she stitches me up.

Polly Pocket

While you are in the shower, I wedge myself into the left-hand pocket of your jeans. It's a tight fit, but with a bit of wiggling I manage to squeeze in and sit crossed-legged, on the internal seam. All through my childhood I tried to fit into the pockets on shirts, aprons and in the deep pockets of jackets. But until now, all I've ever managed was half a leg, or my head. This is the first time I've shimmied the whole way inside a pocket. Your shower is long and steamy and, when you finally start to slip the jeans up your legs, your skin is warm through the fabric. As you step into them, you don't seem to notice they are a little heavier on one side. I'm excited about being with you for the whole day, but on Tuesdays you work late and I wonder if I should have brought some snacks and cola with me. When you sit on the bed to put on your socks, I am flattened against your thigh. It's a snug feeling, like being tucked into bed with stiff sheets. You're running late and as you grab the mug from the bench, you spill milky tea down your pants. I can tell because there's a wet spot next to my arm and some of the tea starts to seep into my hair. Suddenly I'm dropped to the floor and stuffed into the washing basket. I'm surrounded by pockets—in a kind of pocket heaven. I crawl around for a while trying out different pockets for size but I return to the familiarity of your jeans. I take a nap and hope I can get out of the washing basket before the next wash cycle.

Gingerbread man

Not long after you leave, I make a life-sized gingerbread man to replace you. I have to bake him in sections and glue him together with toffee, but he holds together as I lay him out on the kitchen bench. I give him a little check shirt made of icing and a panama hat made out of Rice Krispies with a licorice trim. I've made him spicy, with just enough cinnamon to keep me warm at night. When we cuddle up on the couch, his places his rounded hand on my thigh—I thought about giving him fingers, but he's more submissive without opposable thumbs. When I take him to bed, he moulds himself around me, stroking my hair and whispering sweet things in my ear. I don't complain about crumbs in the bed because in his arms, I dream about peppermint and candy canes. On Christmas Eve he absconds to Coles to hang out with the gingerbread women, liberating them from their plastic wrappers. When he returns, goofy smile on his face, I break him into little pieces and dip his body parts into my milky coffee until he's sludge at the bottom of my Christmas mug. I look at the mixing bowl and start wondering when you'll be back.

Astronaut Ice-cream

At the Smithsonian giftshop, I weigh you down with freeze-dried Neapolitan ice-cream. Pink stripe. Chocolate stripe. White stripe in between—a kind of no-woman's land. Keeping chocberry possibilities at bay. I've never liked the middle band of vanilla ice-cream, have always eaten it last. It reminds me of cheap scented candles or essence in a cake. "Vanilla—like sex on Thursdays," I once said. You didn't laugh. I'm not sure if it was because it was a Thursday. In the National Air and Space Museum you tell me I'll probably be your last lover. And I spend the afternoon worrying about 'probably'. And whether 'probably' means 'possibly', which would make it more possible. Or likely. And why you didn't just say 'likely'. You drag me around the 17,000 space artifacts but you are most interested in the Apollo 11 objects. Buzz's helmet appears to be your favourite, but I'm fascinated with the object labelled 'Pouch, Storage with Roll-on Urine Cuffs' and wonder why anyone would want to keep the 'Fecal Collection Assembly'. You are delighted to find the astronauts left ninety-three bags of poo, pee and puke on the moon, but I don't think that's very friendly—eco or otherwise. You can't say, 'We come in peace' and then leave excrement as your parting gift. We ask the museum curator where we can find the astronaut ice-cream. He tells us it was rejected for flight because it was too crumbly for zero gravity—the astronauts had butterscotch pudding instead. So, I want a refund for false advertising. The man in the giftshop says, "In space, no-one can hear your ice-scream" with a wink, and I say "Probably" and think it's very likely.

PART II

Charnel House

When you left, I wrote a graveyard of prose poems for you. Fragments, half-phrases, broken images; it was as if your closure had made mine unthinkable. So they sit in a folder like bones in a coffin; a menagerie of missing parts waiting for me to bury the remains. But I'm too haunted by wisps of memory and the weight of forgetting to move. My charnel house of prose poems is full of pieces I've tried to stitch together. They are nothing more than a patchwork of words but I still can't lay them to rest.

Blue Heaven

i.

It starts with the tiny ballet shoe earrings you left in the mailbox on my birthday, a rolled-up fragment of script putting words in my mouth; the ones you've been waiting a decade to hear. In the green room of your heart, we slow dance on long starry nights and make love in the bed they used in the previous year's production of *Cabaret*. I'm muse, lover, dancer, poet, angel. Always in that order. I'm the bright spots in your narrative. The thick ink in your pen. At rehearsal, you touch my naked earlobes and notice I've let the holes grow over. You offer to pierce them again with a sterilised needle. I miss seeing myself pressed between your sentences; miss the thrill of finding coded intimacies in your published words. I remember photographs of the moon you sent from your bedroom window. I preferred the new moon while you always liked the last quarter. Eleven of your twenty-one scripts have happy endings. You ask me how this one should finish, but I know from the last time not to give you closure.

ii.

Between the seventh and eighth count, the ribbon on my left pointe shoe comes adrift. I feel the cross of pink satin loosen and the frayed strip inch down my midfoot. I sit downstage and sew a new ribbon into my shoe; the needle and thread moving through the fabric in a familiar rhythm. In the half-light I see you walk down the centre aisle, a giant Slurpee in your hand. You set it down beside me. Mid-stitch, I bend down to take a sip. I know it will be Blue Heaven before the ice is even half way up the straw. I want to tell you in the years since we parted I've been drinking golden pash primas; that the sheets on my bed are no longer lemon and I don't dance to the soundtrack from *Pretty in Pink* when I've had too much to drink. Instead, I tell you Blue Heaven is still my favourite and you take my hand as if the skipped beat is just syncopated rhythm.

iii.

Your friend calls me Cherry Pie; tells me I still remind him of Lana Del Rey and asks me if I am wearing that toe ring with the star on it that you won at the Royal Melbourne Show. He recites the story of the time you taught me snooker while I drank vodka and raspberry through a twisty straw and scored more fouls than you'd both ever seen: Remember when you played a shot balanced on the edge of the table, both feet off the floor? And when you hit the pink ball off the table. I tell him I only remember long Summer nights, your hand stroking the base of my neck as you kissed me to *Chicago*'s 'Entr'acte' on repeat. How, later, I made Fosse moves in your bed while you pulled down my leotard. Your friend tells me you still listen to *Chicago*'s 'Entr'acte' when it rains. I tell him I still have the toe ring.

iv.

This morning I found the necklace you gave me, beneath the faded drawer liner in my nightstand, Tiny Dancer, engraved on the nameplate. It was smaller than I remembered and tarnished after years of resting against the hollow of my throat. In six years, I never took it off. Even after I left you, I wore it like a souvenir of your love; a token of the times you laid me on an old theatre drape on the school's football oval and counted the shadows of stars on my skin. I touch the tiny 'y' curled tightly to fit inside the sterling silver rectangle and think about returning it to my neck. I don't turn it over, but I know there is a heart engraved on the back. The catch is stuck, so I place the clasp between my front teeth and slowly squeeze the link back together.

v.

You bought me eleven things in the first year, but I didn't think to count them until now. I'm still not sure if I should include the Melbourne Uni windcheater you let me keep after you spilt champagne down my dress on Opening Night. Or the white rose you gave me from your lapel when you left the bridal party for rehearsal. Once I told you we left the best part of ourselves in that auditorium. You said the muffled sound of my pointe shoes still haunts the polished boards downstage. I don't tell you I still wear the diamante hairpin you bought me in New York; or that sometimes I imagine how it felt when you slid it into my hair.

Inscription

I'm writing you a poem steeped in deep blue; an ode set against a saxe sunset. Forgive me, it's more blue plate special than blue ribbon ice-cream. A whisper of a poem laps against my chest but I wait for it to swell and shipwreck. It's the lapis of flotsam and jetsam that excite me. Outside the gibbous moon illuminates the blank page. There is a fountain pen of night at my core.

Marginal

You catch my breath as it floats under a room of words; it warms your palms before easing through the spaces between your fingers, rising like a High C. In this snuggery we are a fragment of ourselves; a line without an ending; a gap in the kerning. Between your sheets I am your skin and my heart; an ecstasy of limbs. When I leave your bed, my corpus haunted by your touch, I'm not sure what you will remember and how much time will smooth the edges of our ragged right margin.

Spot

I live in ellipse, between the spots that dot the page. Evenly spaced they hide our transgressions: the imprint of your fingers on my waist; the brush of your soft collar on my neck; my lips urging yours apart. At the end of the page they equivocate on the fullness of time. Some days the triad of circles conceal afternoons of champagne and concupiscence. Sometimes they point to your internal disquietude. You've thought about it one hundred times, a centenary of thought in a matter of weeks and you're back to where we started; with three stuttering dots ahead.

Volcano

In the cooling aftermath, I become glassy rock. My fingers covering the last place you kissed me, sparing it from destruction. Once, I occupied the spaces between your ribs, dwelt in the thick absences between embraces, but broken language ignited a fire that marched beneath my skin. I am more than your pilot light. I am subtle as a volcano. When you find me, there's a pocket of hot air beneath my igneous palm.

Abbey

We sit behind the clock face; the inner workings of the mechanism are exposed. Before electricity, a man sat in this cramped space and protected the Abbey from the lantern's flames. On the crowded bench, your right side presses against my left. A quick fire leaps through my bones. I remember your breath on my collarbone, your hand on my thigh. As you stand and make your way down the stairs, I look at the backwards numbers on the dial and realise if I ignite, there is no-one to extinguish the flames.

Letter

At last my tongue unfurls its vindications. I'm not a silent object of love; a rouged letter in the ruckles of your bed. You try and squeeze me into your glass slippers, but I'm soaring towards the ceiling, crystal shards studding my collarbone. When I write, it's a poem about women and freedom; a familiar letter to Veronica Franco. Together, our words overwrite the roar of accusations and the lapping silence of inequality.

Luna

I'm your woman in white, your agoraphobic poet, your lunatic escapee. On Fridays, your fingers play the air above my spine and the notes vibrate in my solar plexus. I lift my shoulders and your hands inhabit the vacant space. Wordless, I breathe emptiness into your chest. Sometimes when we walk the grid of the city, the backs of our hands brush and we stop mid-step. As you peel back my snow-coloured duffel coat, I'm your Giulia Occhini, pressing the light from between our silhouettes.

Daisy

I'm East Egg, rather than West. Coddled rather than scrambled. I like my soldiers made from rye bread and my butter spread all the way to the crust. On Sundays, I eat my eggs over easy and every so often I give prairie eggs a try. In my white dress, you tell me I look the way you imagine Daisy Buchanan does. But all I can think of is how eggs and daisies are the same colour. You tell me I'm your dream girl, your muse, your holy grail. I tell you I just want to be loved by a man the way Daisy is loved. I think of daisy chains and remember how my nana taught me to make them by splitting their stems with my fingernail and threading them through each other. I cried because it made the flowers die faster. When I say I know you will leave me, I mean that I'm sure I'll be the one to go. I might be your green light at the end of the dock, but I'm also yellow on the inside.

Leucothoe

The sun has my mother's face. Pointed features ringed by a mane of light, she opens her lion's mouth to heat the seed of unease that grows in my belly. In a graveyard in Winchester, you tell me you want to be buried; your body returned to the earth when you die. Every night since then I have laid you to rest; exorcised your touch from my skin; your hands from my hair. The sun reaches into the earth and metaphors begin to rise from the dirt, they flower like wild roses across your headstone. My abdomen swells to triple its size; an enlarged space for my pullulating grief.

Yellow Brick Road

I live in the tall yellow building in your heart. Tower-like, rapunzelled, I wait for you to dislodge me from your upper left chamber, so that I can go home. Inside this lone *Tetris* block, I imagine I am inhabiting part of the yellow brick road; a fragment of golden path from the eastern quadrant in Munchkin County. At sunset, your heart burns a hole in my ruby slippers.

Un

I wake to find no air in my lungs, just the shadow of used words on the ceiling. I think about reaching for them, but no amount of coaxing will return them to my chest. Instead, I watch as they cling like black stars to the tops of the windows; waiting to slip into the night and become someone else's. I try to unthink my thoughts; untype my poems; untouch your skin. But they exist in a space that continues to grow, untamed. So, I wait for you to be my breath, fill my lungs and squander your words on me.

Butcher

If I'd known, I would have taken my time; moved like a shadow in your periphery. If I'd realised, I would have drawn it out, like a large charcoal sketch on butcher's paper. But I sliced through the days like a reaper, anatomising my heart against the backdrop of your sticky words. I recorded our story, until my tightly spun narrative overwrote your desire. Now you tell me I occupy too much of your sight; the centre of your eye is fatigued. In the space between breaths, I imagine my ribs are an empty cage and take a step back.

Eidolon

In the deep forgetting, you take my wrists and plunge them into the ocean. The water level makes an indelible mark on my skin, a liminal place where I begin and end. You say my name underwater and I pitch pole; a commemorative capsizing of allonym and fortuity. As I founder, I see that the foundations of this place are nothing but threshing mudfish. In the deep forgetting, your house is singing you a lullaby; if only you could bury your palm in the sand and seize its last breath.

Boston

for Bay

I've never made a snow angel, never tobogganed or managed to catch your mittened hand when we scurry through the Common. But as the light gathers around us, and the sky ripples nine shades of blue, I stand on the ice and call you to me. You test the ice with every step, the tip of your toe tapping the space before you place your foot. You see the snowflakes in my hair as a veil of stars and kiss my algid lips warm. As I tip my head back, I see ice crystals free-falling; my words become the fine rime on their backs.

Tinker

i.

You called me your Tinkerbell; used a dam to patch my tin heart. I was a bricolage of men's alloyed promises and you rasped and smoothed them down; gave me a satin finish. In your hands, my back was a timpani of bones; my ribs a hollow stock pot. As you tinkered with my scapula, I told you if I was a pan, I'd be a cocotte—so you pulled me on top of you until I boiled over. I asked you to stay, told you my favourite character as a child was always Saucepan Man, but you said you needed to move on—solder someone else's tin heart. I lied and told you I didn't give a tinker's cuss.

ii.

Your hands spanned my ribcage, fingertips digging into the shallow spaces between my bones—leaving red spots on my skin. You were rash. I came down with lover's measles. Your tape measure was a cold strip from collarbone to waist. You measured the circumference of my left ankle; the space between freckles. I measured the breaths between heartbeats; the sighs between espresso shots in green and orange cups. You pushed me against the architrave, balanced a ruler above my head and made a biro mark in the shiny paint. Five feet four in stilettos. Louboutin for the red sole. Soul mate. Like my bleeding heart. I took the tape from your pocket and measured your inner seam. You dressed to the left; my nerve centre throbbed on the right. Naked as an Empress, I was unstitched as you sewed.

iii.

On the last day, I made you chewy Anzac cookies and we watched the sunrise to the stark strains of 'The Last Post'. Apricot light was a soundwave feathering outwards from the horizon. I reached up and removed a stray oat from the corner of your mouth.

iv.

You said I had mermaid hair so I plaited a long, thin strand and placed it around your neck; a peach-coloured garland. I told you I was like Glynis Johns in Miranda; you said I was more tempestuous. An Ariel to your Ahab. A Lorelei to your Sinbad. At night you recited 'The Rime of the Ancient Mariner' while I ate spaghetti marinara and flew around your bedroom like an albatross. But when you turned off the lights I became your siren; a pulsing threnody. Under a canopy of my hair, you stroked my breasts and kissed the dip between my neck and collarbone until I foundered. Before you pulled anchor and sailed away, you said I'd always be your silver girl.

v.

In the late 90s I was your sugar baby; your jam tart. You flew me to Sydney for dinner and to Tahiti on long weekends. On cool nights you covered me with your body. I was your manic pixie dream girl before it was a trope—your Holly Golightly; your Patricia Franchini; your Sugar 'Kane' Kowalczyk. You fed me oysters, caviar and poisson cru and tucked frangipanis behind my right ear—sunset plumeria with pink and yellow stripes. In the morning you watched me stir caster sugar into my cola and eat gummy bears in threes; you said, "Come here and give me some sugar". I reached across and caressed the bottom left part of your ear lobe—a miniature apricot hanging from a golden tree. I ran the pad of my index finger across your lips and licked your cheek. Prickly pear. Custard apple. When you nuzzled my nape you said I smelt like peach fizz; whispered, "Baby peach bubbles" into the dark. But you became hyperglycemic and not even my candy striper outfit was enough to persuade you.

vi.

We bonded over tinned butter beans and homebrand non-fat Greek yoghurt. I had a huge bag of rice in my trolley and you had a sack of unwashed potatoes. I was a kipfler girl, loved the creaminess of their flesh; their waxy finger-shape. You preferred desirees because they reminded you of Tennessee Williams and sultry nights. I liked gratin dauphinoise and fondant potatoes but you preferred hasselback and jacket. I made scalloped and your favourite were mashed. We collided in a cloud of carbohydrates. Hale and hearty. You were all heart; bought Valentine's Day cards in bulk—two decades of I love you for $5.95. You purchased rolls of one-ply toilet paper by the dozen; prawn flavoured two-minute noodles by the pallet. But you were generous in bed and liberal with your kisses; spent your time trailing fingertips between my breasts and paying me compliments. One night, after sex, you ended it by saying I wasn't cheap enough to be a really good deal.

vii.

Your 'please pleases' in the bedroom were polite but insistent. I kissed every spot you implored me to, and slipped my arm across your chest as you slept. When you beseeched me to choose the apple crumble rather than the cherry pie, I acquiesced—even though I hate cinnamon and dislike apples. I watched you drink Glowtinis all night after I gave in to your entreaties to be designated driver. But when you said it would be a mistake to leave you, I begged to differ.

viii.

When you told me you were a cat burglar, I warned you I was an animal activist. You said you didn't steal cats. But I wanted to know where you stashed your felines and what your intentions were. "Pure breeds or tabbies?" "I'm the Cat," you said, "like Cary Grant in *To Catch a Thief.*" You took two velvet cases from a hollowed hardcopy of *The Unbearable Lightness of Being.* The first contained a tennis bracelet; white diamonds on a white gold chain. You clasped it around my wrist. The second box contained a Harry Winston necklace: One hundred and ninety-five marquise and pear-shaped diamonds, weighing a total of 136.66 carats, set in platinum. I lifted my hair and you kissed my nape before securing it around my neck. It was cold and heavy on my collarbone. "What then shall you choose," you asked unzipping my dress, "weight or lightness?" My body heat warmed the platinum; I was an electrical conductor, crackling under your fingertips. Your hot breath misted the diamonds on my décolletage. "Love begins at the point when a woman enters her first word into our poetic memory," you said expectantly. But I remained silent. The following night I was woken by sirens. I got a cat and gave it a diamond collar.

Core

i.

If I could wrap you in my pink bunny rug then you could be my childhood. My Royal Doulton plate. My Bunnykins mug. My Humbert Humbert. I told you I didn't need a father. You told me I had been dating them my whole life. I wanted you to kiss my blue wrist. I just wanted. I was told I should only take what I needed. You remain. That night is there. Looming like The Double Event. That night waits. Throbbing at my core. Always. Taunting me. Revelling in my mistake.

ii.

If I could draw you into my web then you could be my core. My lifeblood pulsating. Flatliner. I could have been your first double figure. I could have had half what you did. Am I just a Mary Kelly to you? Killer heart. Razor sharp.

Leftovers
by Cassandra Atherton

Acknowledgement for poems previously published is made to the following books, journals and anthologies: *Colours: Yellow; Giant Leaps: fifty poets reflect on the fiftieth anniversary of the Apollo 11 moon landing and beyond; Metamorphic: 21st century poets respond to Ovid; Pleasant Troubles; Pre-Raphaelite and other Prose Poems; The Six Senses; The Stony Thursday Book; Stride Magazine; Western Humanities Review.*

First published 2020

POETRY

ISBN: 978-0-6487825-0-6

BOOK, TYPSETTING, AND LOGO DESIGN
Mountains Brown Press

PUBLISHER
Life Before Man

Gazebo Books
PO Box 375
Summer Hill
New South Wales 2130
Australia

gazebobooks.com.au/life-before-man/

2 4 6 8 10 9 7 5 3 1

COVER IMAGE: *Offal*, 2019, oil on canvas, 56 x 40.5 cm, © Phil Day

ISBN 978-0-6487825-0-6

www.ingramcontent.com/pod-product-compliance
Lightning Source LLC
LaVergne TN
LVHW051014080826
845145LV00009B/2609

* 9 7 8 0 6 4 8 7 8 2 5 0 6 *